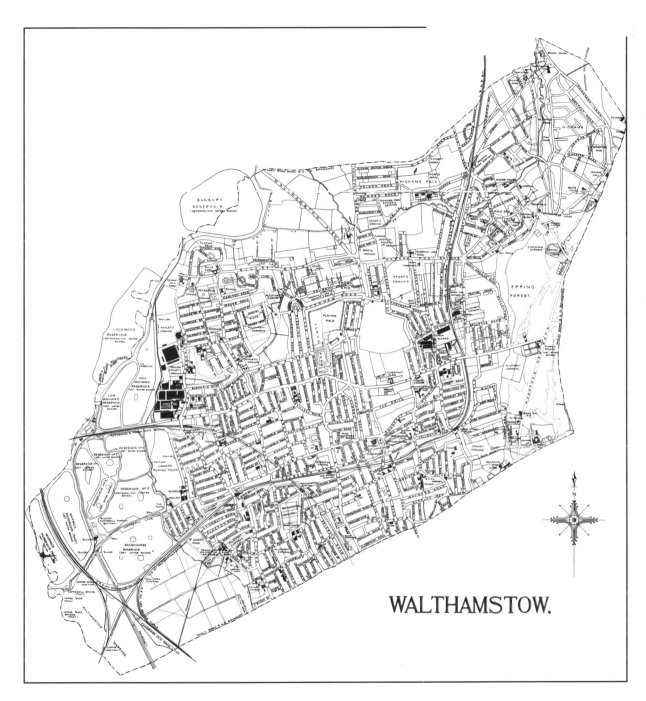

WALTHAMSTOW.

Bygone
WALTHAMSTOW

Hoe Street scene filled with pedestrian shoppers in the 1920s with the *Tower Hotel* on the left.

Bygone
WALTHAMSTOW

Brian Evans

Phillimore

1995

Published by
PHILLIMORE & CO. LTD.,
Shopwyke Manor Barn, Chichester, West Sussex

ISBN 0 85033 967 7

Printed in Great Britain by
BIDDLES LTD.
Guildford, Surrey

Dedicated to all those who pioneered the
Walthamstow Antiquarian Society,
including George E. Roebuck and Annie R. Hatley,
and to Susan, source of inspiration

List of Illustrations

Frontispiece: Hoe Street in the 1920s

Acknowledgements

The author would like to thank the following for the help they have given with the illustrations and information: the Passmore Edwards museum, the Vestry House museum of the London Borough of Waltham Forest and the Walthamstow Antiquarian Society.

Out of the Forest

The story of Walthamstow's development from a group of forest villages into a populous, thriving town with important industrial areas is, in spite of appearances, a romantic one. Significant among the achievements of the 20th-century municipality are the retention of large areas of open ground and woodland, and the preservation of historic areas, notably the old village clustered around the church, and the Vestry House museum where one can picture the pageant of the town's long history in delightfully antique surroundings,

The curtain has been lifted on remote stages in this history through the discovery of artefacts and later descriptions found in documents. Local place-names provide a rich source of information when decoded and related to other information. P.H. Reaney, one of this century's principal researchers into English place-names was a master at the local Monoux School. Reaney examined the early form of the town's name documented in 1067 as 'Wilcumestouue' and showed that this meant 'the welcome place', a name given by the Saxons who appreciated the area's usefulness as a place of resort. The marsh on one side proved good for defence, while the forest provided the means of escape under cover. The higher ground nearby also ensured a good view, particularly in the direction of London as later writers have testified.

Long before the arrival of the Saxons early Palaeolithic and subsequent Neolithic tribes found the edge of the marsh a suitable habitat. During the construction of the Maynard reservoir numerous implements from prehistoric and later eras were unearthed. Some early inhabitants had a very direct relationship with the waterside; they lived in pile-dwellings or 'crannogs' built on platforms raised high above the water level of the river, supported by the up-ended trunks of trees. Presumably these people were skilled fishermen, aware of every mood of their environment. By using boats the settlers could move about easily, communicate with other groups and defend themselves against attackers through their knowledge of the marsh. An ancient dug-out canoe was excavated during the construction of the reservoirs in the Lea Valley, near Walthamstow, and is of a type associated in Europe with lake-dwellings. A so-called 'Viking' boat of plank construction was also discovered during reservoir construction. A Roman settlement has been identified in the area of the *Eagle* at Snaresbrook, and it has been suggested that the Romans used the Lea marshlands for leisure pursuits such as gladiatorial combat. A Roman *contorniate* (circus piece) was discovered during drainage work at Vallentin Road, giving credence to this theory. A Romano-British vase came to light when the Kingfisher pool at Oak Hill was excavated.

And so we move to the fate of Walthamstow after the Norman Conquest. The parish church is first mentioned in a charter of 1108 which granted land to the Priory of Holy Trinity, Aldgate. The site is thought to have been a place of worship since Saxon times however—possibly dating from the time of St Cedd in the seventh century, when he was converting the people of East Anglia. At the time of the Conquest there were two manors, but these were subdivided. The main one was retained by Waltheof, the Saxon Earl of Huntingdon, who was allowed to continue in possession by swearing allegiance to William the Conqueror. Waltheof married Judith, niece of the Conqueror. When Waltheof committed treason and was put to death, his widow retained 'Wilcumstow'. And so the manor passed to the Toni family and became known as Walthamstow Toni. Lying to the north of what was to develop into the town was the manor of Hecham, later known as Higham. The manor of Salisbury Hall, with its village of Chapel End was formed out of Higham in about 1303. Rectory Manor and Low Hall were created out of Walthamstow Toni around 1145 and 1320 respectively. The creation of Rectory Manor resulted from Alice de Toni granting the church of St Mary to the Priory of Holy Trinity Priory at Aldgate.

In Tudor times Walthamstow became the country residence of many famous men—the first of note being George Monoux, who settled at Moons in 1507. He became Lord Mayor of London in 1514-15. About this time the northbound route of Hoe Street (Hoe meaning a ridge) had become established as a major route through the area. Monoux died in February 1544 and in June of the same year his friend and associate, Paul Withypoll, who had lived in Walthamstow since 1527, bought the Rectory Manor from the king. The Withypolls flourished in Walthamstow until the end of the century.

In the 16th century more celebrities moved into the area. Roger Ascham, tutor and Latin secretary to Queen Mary and Queen Elizabeth, lived at Salisbury Hall from 1556 until 1568. It is believed that George Gascoigne, poet, soldier and courtier lived at Thorpe Hall in Hale End Road between 1561 and 1577; he was visited by his stepson the poet Nicholas Breton. Martin Frobisher, the maritime explorer who saw action in battle against the Spanish Armada, owned land around Walthamstow through his marriage to a Withypoll. By the late 16th century the population of the five villages of Hale End, Wood End, Church End, Chapel End and Higham Hill had risen to five hundred.

Shortly after the Restoration of 1660 two famous admirals mentioned in Samuel Pepys' diaries were living in Walthamstow—Sir William Batten and Sir William Penn. Pepys, of course, recorded visits to them. By the time of the first Census in 1801 the area had 3,006 inhabitants. During the 19th century the population continued to rise and by 1851 it was 4,959. Just before this, in 1850, the common fields dating from the Saxon period had been enclosed, and they were soon laid out for housing. Areas were retained, however, for use as allotments and for other recreational purposes, while elsewhere land was set aside for gravel digging.

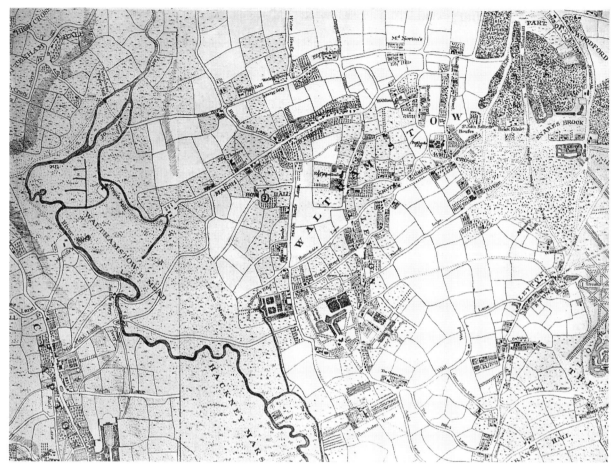

1 John Rocque's map of Walthamstow and its surroundings, 1744. The road at the top right is labelled 'to Walthamstow Windmill' (near Snaresbrook). There are large areas of fields, marsh and the outskirts of the forest. Some of the large mansions are marked, as are the names of landowners. There are many ferries on the river Lea (Green's, Morris's, Smith's and Jeremy's).

2 For centuries important people had found the air and country at Walthamstow congenial. Nicholas Thorne, whose brass of 1546 in the parish church is shown, was a kinsman of Robert Thorne, one of the great triumvirate of Bristol aldermen who put life into Walthamstow during the 15th and 16th centuries. Henry VIII had created the rectory of Walthamstow, and he granted the advowson to Paul Withypoll and his son Edmund in 1544. Paul was a great friend of both George Monoux and Robert Thorne.

3 George Monoux's Grammar School, which he founded in 1527, is seen here from the churchyard. Monoux's friend Thorne had founded a school in Bristol which may have given Monoux the inspiration. This picture dates from 1906.

4 Moon's Farm in Billet Road (formerly Moon's Lane), Moon in this instance being a variant form of Monoux. George Monoux came into possession of the land in 1513, before this date the district had been known as Langland. Later this property came up for sale for development on several occasions and it was finally demolished in 1927, just after these photographs were taken. Monoux Grove identifies the spot today. In the Middle Ages a large moated building was on the site, and by the 17th century it had become a small, timber-framed farmhouse.

5 Moon's Farm barn and pond.

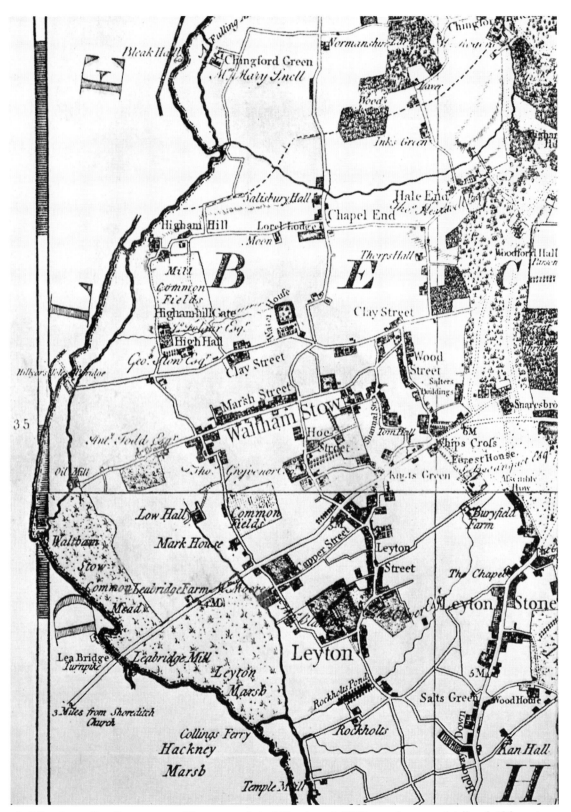

6 Like the earlier Rocque map, Chapman and André's plan of 1777 reveals many details of 18th-century Walthamstow, including the mill near Woodford Hall, Moon's Farm, the remains of the common fields and the buildings along Marsh Street, later the High Street.

7 The parish church from the north west in 1783. The Monoux chantry chapel can be seen on the left, along with the low aisles of the main church which were later raised when the first galleries were installed. Notice the three games players in the churchyard and the digger at work on a grave.

8 (*left and below left*) The Ancient House, Church Lane (before and after restoration), also known as the White House, is the oldest domestic property in the area. There is documentary proof of its existence from 1668. At this time it was held copyhold (a common form of holding in Walthamstow) from the main manor of Walthamstow Toni. In 1908 it formed a row of shops, which included a cycle-maker and dining rooms.

9 (*below*) St Mary's Church in 1904. Not much is left of the pre-Reformation church. It was extensively rebuilt *c*.1535 by Monoux's largesse and with a contribution from Robert Thorne's legacy. Thorne had died in 1532.

10 Grosvenor House, Hoe Street in 1792, one of Walthamstow's country mansions.

11 The Vestry House, home to Walthamstow's local government in the 18th and 19th centuries. It was originally built as the workhouse in 1730 and was enlarged in 1756. This view of June 1932 shows the outline of the roof of the demolished cage on the wall on the left, a place of imprisonment for wrongdoers. The stocks, also used to punish those who had transgressed, formerly stood on the Green.

12　Copper mills were established on the Walthamstow marshes. In 1806 the linseed oil mills were put up for sale, having recently been rebuilt. The British Copper Company bought them two years later in order to roll copper. The business was sold in 1824 to Henry Bath & Co. and in 1832 to Williams, Foster & Co., whilst maintaining the trading name of the British Copper Co. There were 30 hands at work in 1848 but operations ceased in 1857 and in 1896 the East London Waterworks took over the site for use as a pumping station.

13　From *c*.1809-10 until 1814 the British Copper Co. issued 1d. and ½d. copper tokens; such tokens were used as currency in many areas, due to the shortage of coins in national circulation. There was a mint at the mill, but it is believed that much of the rolled copper was sent away to be turned into tokens etc. elsewhere.

14 Tower Hamlets in 1875, from the surrounding fields.

15 Peaceful, sylvan Hoe Street, in sun and shadow, speaks volumes about Walthamstow in 1875. The Red House can be seen in the distance. On the right are the front walls of Court House.

16 Young ladies at play on the water at Shern Hall in 1875.

17 Rectory Manor House was enlarged in 1783 to Sir John Soane's designs; Soane worked on it again in 1791. The Rectory Manor originated when half a virgate and an acre of meadow was given to the Priory of Holy Trinity, Aldgate, in the early 12th century by Alice, daughter of Waltheof. The last house on this site was demolished in 1897 and Howard and Rectory Roads were built.

18 Puddledyke, looking north and showing the field path known to generations of local walkers and anglers near the southern end of the High Maynard reservoir. The construction of the reservoir changed the scenery of Walthamstow marshes.

19 Church Lane, showing the brick cottages next to the church in 1905.

20 View of the old wooden cottages at the bend of Church Lane, 1905.

21   The hamlet of Chapel End, 1905.

22   Cottages at Higham Hill in March 1900.

23 Oak Hill cottages in 1903.

24 Forest country—the bridle path and lodge cottage, Oak Hill, Highams Park.

25 Oak Hill, leading to Woodford New Road and thence to Hale End and Highams Park, 1910.

26 Forest School in 1875. It was set in a picturesque corner of the parish, against the trees, by the Common. These Georgian houses had well-preserved interiors. The school was founded in 1834, in a house in the forest on the edge of the parish boundaries, and it continues to this day.

Growing Pains

27 The Dragon Well dates from the mid-19th century and was 'erected on the forest'. Early attempts to improve the facilities of Walthamstow usually stemmed from the benevolence of the local gentry. Many areas of the town suffered from inadequate water supplies—a factor which played its part in the ill-health and limited life-span of the poorer sections of society.

"THE DRAGON WELL" AT WALTHAMSTOW.

THE subject of this Illustration derives interest, as well for its rarity in modern days, and for the liberality of the donor, as for its intrinsic merit and usefulness. It has recently been erected on the Forest, at Walthamstow, from the design of Mr. G. E. Pritchett, of Bishop Stortford, architect, through the liberality of a neighbour, whose object was to provide with water a poor neighbourhood hitherto unsupplied. The whole is beautifully executed in Caen stone, by Mr. Rattle, of Cambridge. An eagle's head forms the spout, and above is an iron lamp, of pleasing design. The basin is of oak, slightly ornamented. In the carved panels is inscribed :—" Jesus said, whosoever drinketh of this water shall thirst again, but whosoever drinketh of the water I shall give him shall never thirst, but the water that I shall give shall be a well of water springing up to everlasting life." Under the carved work at the top is inscribed :—" Ho every one that thirsteth, come ye to the waters." The popular name is derived from the dragon sculpture.

28 The Town Hall is photographed here in 1910. The conversation between the two men has been interrupted by the arrival of the photographer. The local board of health took over from the vestry; it had 12 members until 1891 when the number was increased to eighteen. The board met in the Vestry House until 1876 when the public hall in Orford Road (built in 1866) was bought and enlarged for use as a town hall. Another wing was added in 1890-1. The front of the building survived as part of the Connaught Hospital.

29 The fire station, *c*.1904. This new station in the High Street, opposite Storey, replaced the one in Willow Walk in 1895.

30 This 'Wren'-style building is the central library built in 1909. The provision of the library added to the growing facilities offered by the High Street. The founding of the Walthamstow Antiquarian Society, which has done so much to rescue the records and history of the area, was closely associated with the public library and its librarian between 1907 and 1946, George Roebuck.

31 The cover of the sale brochure for Moon's Farm and other properties at Higham Hill, from 17 July 1884. The pace of development was beginning to accelerate.

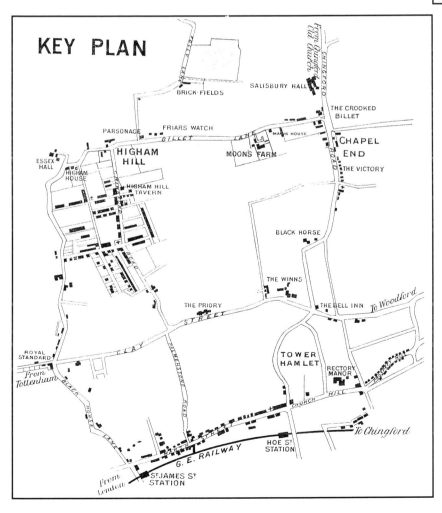

KEY PLAN

32 Key plan for the sale of the brickfields, the Rectory Manor, Tower Hamlets and Chapel End, with an indication of the existing buildings.

33 In 1912 Moon's Farm was again offered for sale, along with the folly in Folly Lane, Walthamstow.

Particulars.

LOT ONE
(Coloured BROWN on Plan).

The Valuable

FREEHOLD PROPERTY,

Situate only a few minutes' walk from the Electric Tram Car Route in the Chingford Road, giving access to all parts of the district and to Hoe Street Station on the G.E.R., whence there is an all-night service of trains to the City, and workmen's tickets are issued at 2d. the return journey,

KNOWN AS

"Moon's Farm,"

Comprising old-fashioned 5-roomed Farm House, Barn, Stables, Out-buildings, Garden, &c., and pasture land, in all containing an area of about

10 Acres,

and possessing a frontage of about 760 feet towards

BILLET ROAD, WALTHAMSTOW.

The property immediately adjoins land now in active development by the Warner Estate Company, and is eminently suitable for

COTTAGES OR FACTORIES
or for
RECREATION PURPOSES.

It is at present let on a yearly tenancy to Mr. J. S. Smith at a rental of £45 per annum, and the last payment of tithe upon the land amounted to about £1 18s. 3d.

The property is sold subject to the rights (if any) of the Epping Forest Commissioners in the open waste land (coloured YELLOW on plan) between the road and the property.
There is a public sewer in Billet Road.

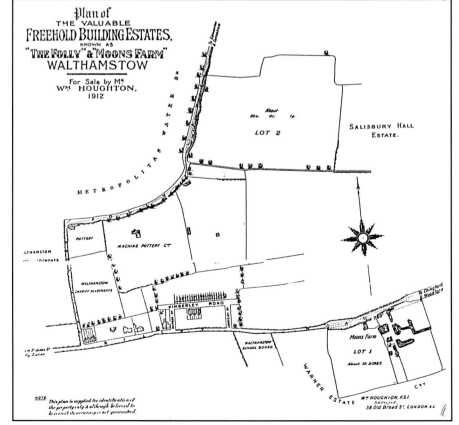

34 The map in this 1912 prospectus gives more interesting detail.

35 In 1909 Warner Estates advertised in a London County Council booklet listing workmen's tram times, evening classes, workmen's dwellings and trade schools.

36 The Beech Hall estate office of Mr. O.H. Watling, builder. This was erected in 1905 on the site of the Regal Cinema, Highams Park, around the corner from Beech Hall Road proper.

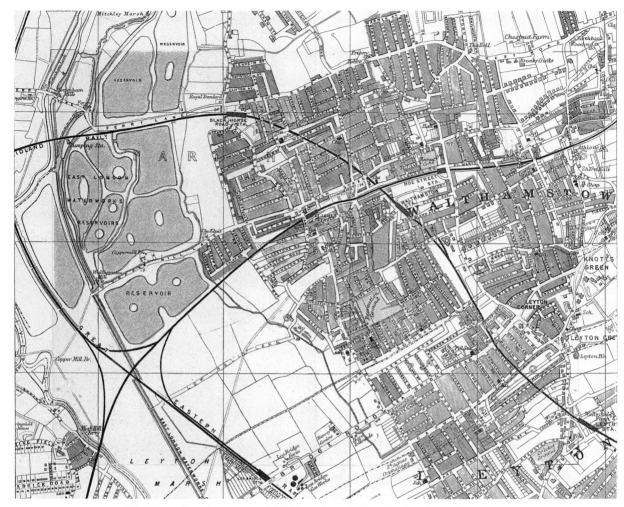

37 Map of west and central Walthamstow, 1905, showing the built-up area.

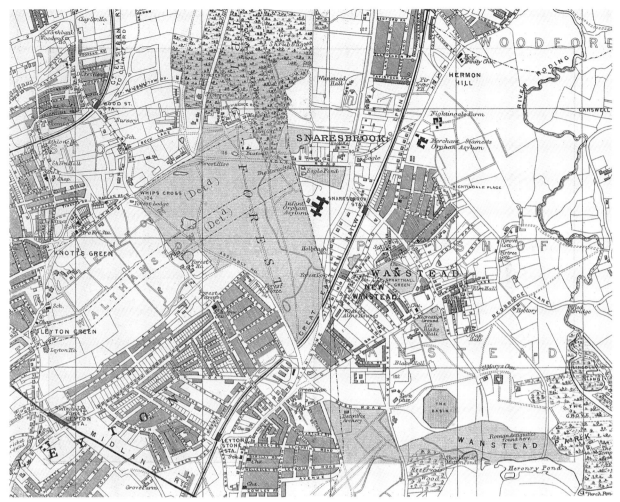

38 Map of north and east Walthamstow, with Snaresbrook and Wanstead to the east. This too dates from 1905.

DATED 27th May 1903.

ELM HOUSE ESTATE WALTHAMSTOW.

Mr. ARTHUR DOYLE and another

TO

Mr. A. ATTWELL.

(COUNTERPART)

Lease

No. 286 Forest Road Walthamstow Essex.

Commences 24th June	-	-	-	1898
For years	-	-	-	99
Expires 24th June	-	-	-	1997

Rent £6 10s. 0d.

The Plan referred to.

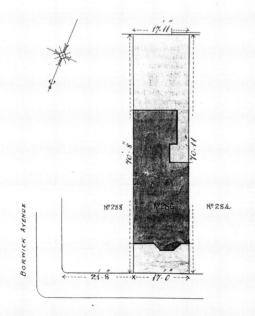

Dated 28th May 1903

Mr Adolphus Attwell

to

Mess.rs Doyle & Lea

Mortgage

of

Leasehold property situate N.º 288 Forest Road Walthamstow Essex subject to a prior Mortgage.

Dated 23rd October 1906

Messrs Doyle & Lea

to

Mr A. Attwell

Surrender

39 The development of Forest Road—(*above*) a mortgage for no. 288 and (*left*) a lease for no. 286; both were part of the Elm House Estate.

40 Early days at the Garden Village, Highams Park, with a forested area in the distance, *c*.1905.

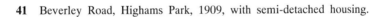

41 Beverley Road, Highams Park, 1909, with semi-detached housing.

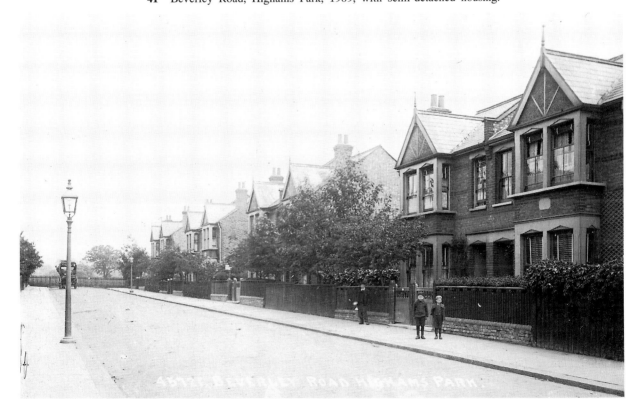

42 (*right*) Terraced houses in Wilton Road, Highams Park.

43 (*below left*) Charles Jones, family butcher, Wood Street at the turn of the century. The ground on which the shop was built was originally part of the Money-Wigram estate.

44 (*below right*) Cox and Sons, drapers, in the High Street, typify the newer style of commercial premises as they advertise their '1st great sale in 20 years'. The photograph was taken in 1913 by Emile Matioli, whose premises were at 76 High Street, opposite the Salvation Army Citadel.

45 The horse-drawn pantechnicons of F. Barrett, removers and warehousers of Hoe Street and Stamford House, Highams Park, are ready to move off, loaded to the gunwales.

46 A Wallis and Steevens traction engine in the service of the firm of Balls, fat and waste contractors of Chapel End, 1908.

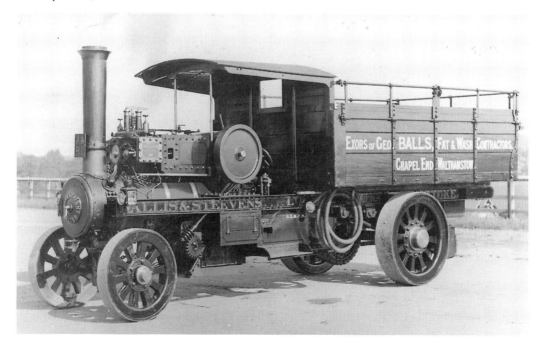

47 The British Xylonite Company's works, Highams Park, during the First World War. In 1896, British Xylonite bought the 50 acres of Jack's Farm at this spot and opened their factory in 1897. The company pioneered the production of celluloid in Britain; but this was superseded in 1921 by lactoid, a non-inflammable substitute. At one time the firm almost had a complete monopoly in the manufacture of table-tennis balls, with the trade name 'Halex' known all over the world.

48 Walthamstow was also home to some of the first film studios—this is Broadwest studio in 1915.

49 The *Royal Oak* at Hale End had been opened in 1906 and this view was taken less than ten years later. It shows a still leafy suburb which was slowly developing.

50 The lodge at Queen's Road cemetery, *c*.1910. With the growth in population there was a need for additional facilities for burials; cremation had not yet become fashionable.

51 A walk in Lark's Wood, 1911. This area on the Chingford borders was a popular resort, but it too attracted developers after the First World War, when its famous Lido swimming pool was built.

52 The Lea Valley to the west of Walthamstow underwent a remarkable transformation between 1863 and 1917, as shown by this aerial view of the reservoirs, taken in 1920.

Walthamstow Reservoirs

No. 1		19 acres	
No. 2		13 acres	These five were filled in between
No. 3		12 acres	1863 and 1866
No. 4		30 acres	
No. 5		41 acres	
No. 6	Racecourse Reservoir	59 acres	Filled in January 1873
No. 7	West Warwick	34 acres	These two were constructed
No. 8	East Warwick	43 acres	between 1895 and 1897
No. 9	High Maynard	38 acres	Both were filled in 1870
No. 10	Low Maynard	25 acres	
No. 11	Lockwood	74 acres	
No. 12	Banbury	91 acres	Constructed soon after 1897
No. 13	King George		Partly over the border, constructed between 1908 and 1917

Wheels through Walthamstow

Among the memories of old Walthamstow which are gathered together in the volume *Across the Years* (ed. A. Hatley, 1953) there are several which show the gradual growth of local transport facilities in the second half of the 19th century. The following is typical:

> Mr. Gilbert Houghton who was born in 1852 in Wood Street has told us that it was just a village street, with large houses at both ends and cottages and small shops on the west side. Pamphion's Nursery and green fields occupied the greater part of the east side. The coach with four horses, run by Mr. Francis Wragg (an old Brighton coachman of some renown) ran from the *Eagle* at Snaresbrook to the Royal Exchange in London via Walthamstow and took businessmen to the city. It came rattling down Wood Street morning after morning, wet or fine. We used to be on the watch for it ... and father, prepared for all weathers, would sally forth and join it at the corner of Wyatt's Lane.

The Wraggs had been coachmasters for four generations, from 1764 until 1870. Dwellers in the forest hamlets around Walthamstow benefited from their enterprise, especially those locals who were employed in the City. In 1836 the drill was to book one's seat at Robert Wragg's coaching office adjacent to the *Chequers* inn in Marsh Street (which was later to become the High Street). At this period the yellow coaches left the *Nag's Head* at Church End eight times a day, with a capacity of 18 passengers. From Church End the coach passed through the sylvan delights of Marsh Street, Markhouse Road, Lea Bridge Road and thence to the Royal Exchange in the City, where the Walthamstovians would descend with a sense of purpose for their day's work. Whatever the pressures the day might bring in bank or counting house, they knew that at the end of the day they would be whisked back to the serenity of rural Walthamstow.

The Wraggs were not been the only coach operators in the forest hamlets. *Paul Pry,* a scandal sheet appearing in 1840, comments as follows:

> There is no harm in Wragg, the coachmaster, starting an omnibus, if he did not interfere with the time of a poor widow, who has a far greater right on the road than he has ... endeavouring to oppress and ruin a widow, who has no other means of subsidence than the profits of the coach he is now hoping to run off the road ...

Bearing in mind that the year 1840 also marked the opening of the railway station at Lea Bridge, just south of Walthamstow, by the fledgling Eastern Counties Railway, one might suspect that this was an attempt to discredit Wragg's attempt to run a service to the station. As such it represented the first warning shot across the bows for coach traffic in the area. However, it was to be 30 years before Walthamstow gained its own railway station—an innovation which sliced through the landscape and changed it for ever.

In between 1840 and 1870 those travellers from Walthamstow who used the Lea Bridge station were mainly the well-to-do locals with City business interests. Many of the older inhabitants, and even some of the younger ones, were nervous or 'chary' of the 'new-fangled' locomotion, since many books and articles had claimed that the human frame was not meant to be whirled forward at such speeds. This belief gave the coaches an extended life until, inevitably, the navvies moved in during the mid-1860s. They began the construction of embankments and cuttings for a branch of the Great Eastern Railway (successor to the Eastern Counties), at a time when an ambitious programme of suburban lines was being promoted. The plan was to link north-east London with a magnificent new terminus at Liverpool Street. Up to this point the railway had only run to an inadequate station named Bishopsgate, which was some way short of the City and nearer to Shoreditch.

In order to profit from this improved communication with London, local developers such as James Higham began to draw up plans for superior housing estates, which would combine the benefits of Walthamstow's relative calm with convenient access to the City. An example of such a project was Higham's Fitzwarren estate. However, one of the consequences of the railway's development in this direction was in fact an influx of the poorer classes, whose homes had been demolished as part of the vast construction works at Liverpool Street Station. In compensation these people were offered cheap housing along the new railway lines in places such as Walthamstow, and reduced fares on trains.

Having begun the new lines the Great Eastern Railway suddenly found itself embarrassed by a lack of sufficient capital and backing from its shareholders. All building work stopped, and in Walthamstow a mile-long embankment offended the eye to the west of St James' Street. The prospect that the railway might fail to reach Walthamstow put the local building developers into a terrible panic. Their agreements often specified completion of houses within a specified time and they doubted that tenants would be found for any of them without the existence of the railway to carry them to work. A deputation led by James Higham went to the railway company in order to try to resolve the impasse. Eventually the line was completed and opened as far as Shernhall Street. The housing work was given a particular impetus by the introduction of cheap fares for early morning workers, and the final section of the line to Hale End and Chingford was completed between 1870 and 1873. Of course, most of the houses built in this era were for rent and not sale. Some of the landlords built up amazingly large 'empires' of rented property including, of course, Thomas Courteney Warner.

53 An accident which occurred in the vicinity of Gosport Road bridge in 1887 led to this locomotive plunging off the embankment.

54 Hoe Lane railway station seen among the fields, *c*.1875.

55 A later view of the Hoe Street platform and commuters in the heyday of rail, 1905. The background now resembles a northern industrial town with its mix of housing and factories.

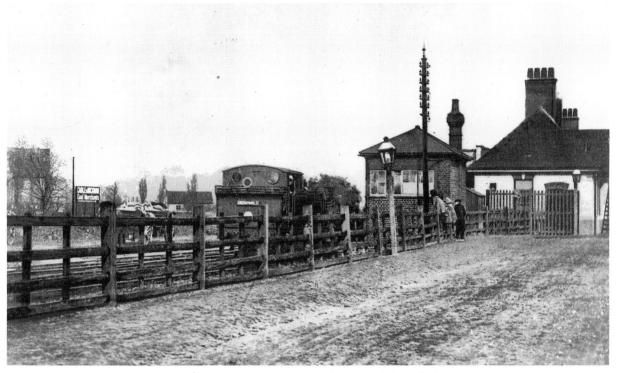

56 The primitive station buildings and wooden fence at Highams Park early this century.

57 An Edwardian passenger leaves Highams Park station, *c.*1905. The posters advertise excursions to Clacton and Alexandra Palace.

58 (*left*) The level crossing at Highams Park in 1905, with the Xylonite factory in the background and a pile of loose chippings to the left. Although there are plenty of people around, time seems to be passing slowly

59 (*below left*) The growing suburb of Highams Park, near the railway station, 1912.

60 (*below right*) A horse tram belonging to the Lea Bridge, Leyton and Walthamstow Tramway negotiating Leyton High Road, *c*.1897.

61 A horse tram leaves the Walthamstow section at Bakers Arms junction.

62 An early vehicle at the *Bell Inn*, Chingford Road in around 1900 performs the function of a bus.

63 The glittering splendour of the official opening of Walthamstow Corporation's electric tramway system on Saturday 3 June 1905. Six cars toured the system—the leading car was driven by Councillor Wilkes. The procession, with the two leading cars decorated and illuminated, then returned to the depot for refreshments.

64 The workforce proudly stand by and on eight of the 32 cars which had been ordered from Brush Electrical of Loughborough.

65 An open-top Walthamstow car en route for Lea Bridge Road terminus is pictured here at the junction with the Leyton Tramways system, at the *Crooked Billet* public house. Note the street furniture.

66 Tramcar no. 20 at Forest Road. The *Royal Standard* was on the route of the Woodford to Ferry Lane service.

67 A fine study of the driver and conductor of the no. 22 bound for Chingford Mount, with repetitive advertising on the risers of the stairs to the top deck.

68 A scene in Chingford Road, 1908.

69   By the tea gardens, Ferry Lane, a covered top car waits to start its return journey.

70   During the First World War women drivers made their first appearances on Walthamstow's trams.

71 Three trams and a service vehicle at Walthamstow depot.

72 'This Car Has Cushion Seats and Pullman Comfort, Try It', reads the slogan on the side of a route 57 Liverpool Street to Walthamstow tramcar. This was part of a modernisation intended to attract customers.

73 A Walthamstow car at Blackhorse Lane about 1937 after the system had been absorbed into the London Passenger Transport Board's operation.

74 A London County Council tram at Hoe Street in 1933.

75 (*above*) The solid-tyred vehicle on the right is a Walthamstow-bound bus on route 38b at its terminus at the *Crown Inn,* Loughton.

76 (*right*) A lively shopping scene in Hoe Street in the 1920s, with a no. 38b bus approaching on its way to Victoria station.

77 (*above*) Bakers Arms junction in the late 1920s with trams and buses competing for passengers.

Walthamstow Market and the High Street

Like many others I have fond memories of visiting the High Street market; in my case they date from my childhood in the years following the Second World War. The feature that sticks in my mind is the cheap confectionery stall with its array of tempting sweet things, particularly coconut ice—a sugary concoction in vanilla and strawberry flavours, samples of which we always carried home with us. Chocolate and other sweet delights were still on ration and in short supply, so these cheap substitutes filled a real need as most Britons in those days had a very sweet tooth. The other memory is of a heady hustle and bustle with the never-ending shouts of the stallholders advertising their wares. There was always the possibility that we might visit a variety show at the Palace Theatre—I think these must have been matinée performances—before we made our way home to Stoke Newington on the bus. I think my mother was attracted to these markets, for we were frequent visitors to others such as that at Ridley Road in Dalston, by their liveliness and the way they reminded her of her childhood in the East End.

The long descent of the road forming the market, which was much narrower than traditional markets but extended for a considerable distance, had originally been the old route down onto the Lea Marshes. Hence its original name of Marsh Street, right up to Hoe Street. From the Chapman and André map of 1777 and the earlier plan by Rocque, the beginnings of development on this site may be charted. This early growth produced some attractive Georgian houses, which have since been despoiled by the 20th century's lack of appreciation for proportion and style. In spite of this development the street remained very open for much of its length with broad fields and, at its lower end cultivated marshlands, even as late as the 1870s.

There is real romance in some of the former history of this land leading to the Lea Marshes. At the marsh end was a house in the fields called The Elms. This was reputed to have been Prince Rupert's lodging on a visit to Walthamstow. At the time he was Master of the King's Ordinance and had come to the powder mill nearby to examine the advances in gunpowder manufacture. At the lower end of the High Street proper stood the house of Richard Abbey, the guardian of John Keats and his sister, Fanny. Fanny actually lived here and attended the 'Academy for Young Ladies' close by. Keats occasionally visited his guardian when his health allowed. We can imagine him making the effort, passing along the then country street, pausing from time to time to catch his breath or cough. Somewhere further up High Street was the house belonging to Admiral Sir William Penn, father of the founder of the state of Pennsylvania. Samuel Pepys, the diarist, was a visitor to this house. Pepys also visited Sir William Batten, the Surveyor to the Navy at his house in Walthamstow. On one occasion, Pepys joined Penn in his two-horse chariot and raced against Batten's coach and four from London to Walthamstow—a quite hair-raising experience in which Pepys ended up muddying his new velvet coat!

In Pretoria Avenue, off the High Street, the Clock House which was built in 1813 by Thomas Courteney Warner replaced the former Black House (the origin of Black Horse Road through alteration in common parlance). The Clock House, like its predecessor, once had outstanding views towards London over the Lea.

Before and in the early days of the market, the High Street was an area with many old-style tradesmen such as plumbers and carpenters. There was also a contractor named Cornell who provided horses and carts under contract, many of them being used for council work. The market did not begin until the early 1880s when costermongers were attracted to the street and began to set up stalls. The local board was not in favour of this development, but the shopkeepers found that they stimulated trade and as a result they were gradually accepted; the board drew up regulations to control their activities and regulate their stalls.

Once the market began to thrive it was crowded from early morning until very late at night—hours of opening were long in those days. Fridays and Saturdays were the principal days. Tempting smells wafted from all along the street. The fast food of the era, although not known as such, was the type of fare available from a German butcher. Two longish trestle tables would be placed outside a shop and then be covered in an immaculate white cloth. Standing on this would be gleaming chromium urns from which hot saveloy sausages, pease-pudding, faggots, black pudding and pigs trotters were dispensed by the butcher in white apron and straw hat. These delicacies would provide the supper for many a local household, saving the money on fuel for the cooking range and making time for other jobs to be done. The evening stalls would each sport a naptha lamp fixed to a hook above the goods, shedding a strong light and creating an interesting spectacle when combined with the roaring noise of the burning fuel. A popular soft drink of the day was sarsaparilla which was dispensed from a large van, parked near the public library. Adult males formed the main clientèle of the *Chequers* public house, although there were some women that could put away beer as fast as most men—the hard times created these Amazons—and fights between women were not uncommon.

These fights provided entertainment for the onlookers. Before the arrival of the Palace Theatre in 1903 there were many forms of spectacle to keep the local people amused. Old inhabitants remembered Bostock's circus camping at the top end of the High Street in what were then fields surrounding the house where the library now stands. Simple entertainments took place; older people in the early 1950s remembering the 19th century recalled a small boy jumping through hoops at the junction of High Street and St James' Street. There was also an address in the High Street known as Bell's Booths, where boxing matches took place.

The long-running fair at the rear of the Salvation Army Citadel provided a rather rumbustious and noisy entertainment, indeed it seemed strange to many that it was not suppressed earlier. Finally there were other musical spectacles to fill people's days with sounds: the Italian hurdy-gurdy players, often accompanied by boys who begged for coppers which had to placed in a bag held by a small rhesus monkey, the German bands (which tended to station themselves at the corner of Pretoria Avenue) and buskers with mobile harmonium.

In the following directory of the High Street in 1890 there are surprising numbers of tradesmen of the same type. In an age when people walked great distances to work, to visit people or to shop, a large number of traders involved with footware is easier to explain than what appears to be an over-provision of cheesemongers. Shoeing-smiths, saddlers and corn dealers hint at the old agricultural scene which was becoming obsolete. Three social clubs make it clear that the High Street had become the place to go to enjoy oneself, and other sources mention rescue and mission work carried out among single women, who appeared to be frequenters of the Market area.

An A-Z of High Street Businesses, 1890

Name	Occupation	Name	Occupation
Andrews & Co.	Ironmongers	Ling, Thomas P.	Grocer
Archer, William Henry	Bootmaker	Lofts, William	Wine and spirit retailer
Bennett (Mrs.) Emily	Butcher	Thomas A. Scrivener, Manager	London & South Western Bank Ltd.
Bishop, Richard	Tripe dresser		
Blackwell, Edward	Confectioner	McDowall, Peter	China dealer
Boggis, Ebenezer	Grocer	Machon, George	Shoemaker
Brailey, Thomas	Draper	Manders, Victor	Photographer
Brittain, Thomas	Grocer and Agent	Marcus, E. & Co.	Furniture dealer
Brown, Charles	Butcher	May, John	Shoe warehouse
Bruckland, Richard	Marine Stores	Maysent, Martin	Fruiterer
Bugg Dowman Gilson	Boot Warehouse	Milbourne, John	Tobacconist
Burbidge, H. & Co.	Confectioner	Miller, Henry	Tinplate worker
Burton, Charles	Butcher	Miller, William	Butcher
Calver, Charles (jr.)	Coach builder	Rev. H.A. Allpas, Headmaster	Monoux Grammar School
Camp, (Miss) Selina	Dairy	Moss, S & Co.	Drapers etc.
Cardo, James & Son	Boot makers & leather sellers	Neal, William	Fancy draper
Carruthers, Thomas	Ironmonger	Nethersole, Arthur George	Ham/Beef dealer
Cattermull, Jonathan	Tailor	Nicholls, John	Tobacconist
Chaplin, Charles	Beer retailer	Nicholson George James	Tobacconist
Cheshire, Thomas	Greengrocer	C.E. Kirk, Superintendent	North London Certified Industrial Truant School
Cheshire, Thomas (jr.)	Fruiterer		
Cobden, George	Watchmaker	Norwood & Bass	Butchers
Cole, Robert	Grocer	Oakes, Thomas Edward	Bootmaker
Collen, Arthur Danby	Baker	Osborne (Mrs.) Hannah	Tobacconist
Coulston, Richard Felton	Ironmonger	Palmer, Charles	Grocer
Dawson, William	Printer	Pettit, Robert W.	Dairyman
Dowler, George	Coffee house	Poore, Thomas W.	Upholsterer
Dye, A.H. & A.W.	Corn chandlers	Popplewell, Joseph	Milliner
Edwards, Alvan H.	Watchmaker	Poupard, Sarah	Dressmaker
Ellison, William James	Stationer	Price & Co.	Tailors
Elves, Alfred	Butcher	Price, William	Baker and post office
Escott, George	Bootmaker	Rabson, William	Grocer
Fish Brothers	Pawnbrokers	Reed, Alfred	Glass and china dealer
Fisher, George	Leather seller & boot maker	Reeves, John	Sewer contractor
Floyd (Mrs.) Ellen	Wardrobe dealer	Rivett, Ebenezer	Oilman
Forbes, (Miss) Edith	Fancy repository	Rose, George	Wardrobe dealer
Ford, William	Confectioner	Sanders, Charles, R.	Cheesemonger
Fyson, Edmund	Surgeon	Saunders, Arthur	Chemist and druggist
Gaydon, H. & E.	Pawnbrokers	Savage, James	Hosier
Gibbs, Charles Rudd	Cheesemonger	Saville, W. & Co.	Music warehouse
Gilbey, W. & A.	Wines and spirits	Siddall, John Robert	Tobacconist
Gilburt, William Henry	Oilman	Simmonds (Mrs.) Rebecca	Milliner
Gouldstone, John	Fruiterer	Skelton, Richard & Son	Vetinerary surgeons
Green, Edmund	Bootmaker	Smith, James	Corn chandler
Groome, Richard William	Shoemaker	Stebbing, John	Draper
Hall, Edmund	Pawnbroker	Stocks, Frederick	Chimney sweep
Hall (Miss) Rachael	General draper	Streitberger, George	Pork butcher
Hallows, William G.	*Chequers* public house	Sutton, George	Surgeon
Harknett, Walter G.	Hairdresser	Swaby, T.H.	Draper
Harris, Samuel	Cheesemonger	Taylor, Oliver	Cheesemonger
Harwitz Bros.	Picture frame makers	Teale, Charles & Co.	Domestic machine dealer
Hastings, George	Shirts and collars	Toynbee, Arthur	Butcher
Mrs. Mary Parsons, Lady Superintendent,	Home for Orphan and Destitute Girls, Eastfield House	Tozer & Co.	Toy dealer
		Tucker, Joseph	Corn dealer
How, J. & Sons	Building material dealers	James Evans, Secretary	Unionists' Social Club
Kearley & Tonge	International Tea Dealers	Upton, Thomas	Butcher
James James & Co.	Tea Dealers	John Cropley, Hon. Sec.	Walthamstow Conservative Club
Jeffery, Edwin	Bootmaker	Ward, Charles James Berrill	Photographer
Jones & Son	Lamp dealers	Watson, William	Shoeing smith
Kempster, Thomas	Saddler	Wells, Edward Thomas	Glass and china dealer
King, Henry	Fishmonger	Weston, William	Confectioner
Kitteridge, R.	Furniture dealer	Wheeler, Joseph	Chemist and druggist
Knightbridge, Henry	Butcher	White (Mrs.) Maria	Cheesemonger
Kurtz, Adolph	Baker	Wieland, Gottlieb	Pork butcher
Lee & Terry	Tailors	E. Saunderson, Secretary	Working Men's Club & Social Institute
Lee (Miss) Ada	Dressmaker		
Lee, Edwin	Butcher	Worton, Thomas	The *Cock* public house
Leeson, Fred	Cheesemonger	Wyeth, Sophia	Dressmaker

78 In Blackhorse Road milk churns are being rolled across the road near the corner of Hazelwood Road, while a horse bus passes northwards. It is early in the reign of George V, and advertising is becoming rampant on the sides of the houses—note the giant hand pointing downwards from the chimneypots on the left.

79 Hoe Street in 1900 with the *Bridge House* tavern prominent on the right. The trams had not then arrived in Hoe Street.

80 By 1908 the trams have arrived in Hoe Street.

81 A busy shopping day in Hoe Street. Charles E.H. Brown's printing and stationery business is at no. 209 on the left behind the *Standard*. A horse and cart is emerging from the alley just beyond. The comment on the back of the photograph reads, 'this portion of Hoe Street is just a little way before Hoe Street Station. Very much improved during the last few years'.

82 Not much room on the pavement and a very muddy roadway in Hoe Street before the First World War.

83 Whitfields' three shops at nos. 294, 296 and 298 Hoe Street in 1910 advertise dresses, blouses and mourning wear. The latter formed an important branch of trade in the days of large families, high child mortality and, for many, poor living conditions.

84 High Street, looking uphill towards the Palace Theatre from the *Chequers* public house, at the corner of Storey Road.

85 The Palace Theatre, Walthamstow, in the High Street pictured in 1905 with one of the earliest buses. The Palace was opened in 1903, closed in 1954 and was demolished in 1960.

86 The High Street, 1908. Marsh Street Congregational church retained the original name of the
street. It was rebuilt in 1871 and remained opposite the central library until 1965. Marsh Street
changed its name to High Street in 1882; it had been a thoroughfare lined with cottages and houses
for many years before the market came. Shops have been built on the front gardens of the houses
behind the church.

87 St James' Street with the station bridge in the background in 1908. The shops are thriving. On the corner Sainsbury's advertises its other stores in the neighbourhood, whilst a dining room specifically mentions that it caters for cricket and football teams. A dentist has taken up residence above the shops on the left.

88 A delightful view taken from the other side of St James' Street station bridge showing the local shopping area just before the First World War.

89 A quiet day in Wood Street by the post and telegraph office, 1908. R. Snaith and Sons at nos. 154 and 156 unusually combined the trades of tailor and stationer, whilst also running the post office.

90 The bend in the road by Wood Street station. J.S. Davies at no. 176, in the centre of the picture, offers to buy furniture, remake bedding and clean venetian blinds. An early road sign warns motorists to drive slowly.

91 (*right*) Thomas Henry Percival was another shopkeeper who ran a strange combination of businesses—a chemist at no. 142 High Road and a cycle agent at no. 140. These sandwich-board men with the strange hats are taking part in an early advertising extravaganza for the Auxeto Gramophone in 1908.

92 (*below*) Bell Corner, *c*.1914, with two buses crossing the junction. One of Walthamstow's nine cinemas at this period, the original 'Electric Theatre', is on the right.

93 (*below*) The Highams Park Electric Theatre advertises the *Battle of Pottsburg Bridge*— 'Holds you Breathless'. The cinema was built in 1911, and this view dates from 1915. Below the cinema is an estate office, across the road are a butcher's and tearooms.

HALE END ROAD, HALE END

94 Church Hill in 1905 was a place where the pedestrian could amble in the roadway without fear of being run over.

95 Prospect Hill, lined by trees and with a solitary street lamp in view, was the place for ladies to chat on their way back from shopping, 1908.

96 In First Avenue, off Hoe Street, saplings supported by a stake have been planted in an effort to make a pleasing avenue of trees. This picture dates from 1908.

97 A fine view of St Saviour's Church, Markhouse Road. The church is remarkable for it was the only Walthamstow church to survive unscathed the great days of the Gothic Revival. Rather splendid too, as reminders of Victorian and Edwardian street furniture, are the elaborate lamp standard on the left and the tram wire pole on the right, which serve to frame the architecture.

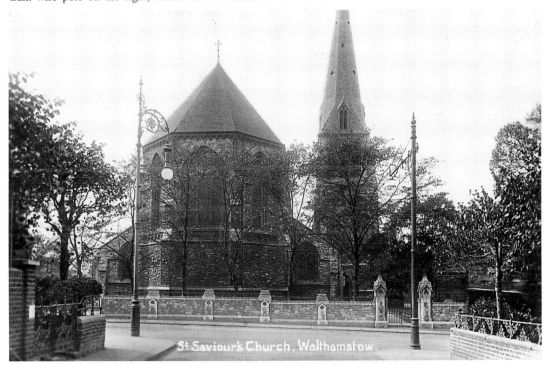

St Saviour's Church, Walthamstow.

98 Livingstone Road, Walthamstow, near the Leyton boundary, in the era of venetian blinds, net curtains and no traffic whatsoever, 1911.

99 A young man at the gate of a Walthamstow house; what did he grow up to become? An interestingly elaborate style of terraced house with a tremendous amount of added decoration and detail, such as roof crown tiles, bargeboards, stucco door and window surrounds with foliage and mythical decoration, a coloured and patterned tile path to the front door which has a recessed porch and coloured glass panes. Note also the front railings. The photograph dates from 1910.

100 Lloyd Park, the Lawn, *c.*1911. Lloyd Park was opened in 1900, after the family of Edward Lloyd (1815-90) had given Water House (also known as Winns, and once the home of William Morris) and nine-and-a-half acres of ground, on condition that the Urban District Council bought the adjoining nine-and-three-quarter acres.

101 The Terrace, Lloyd Park, *c.*1913. The Globe sundial came from a big house north of Walthamstow and was removed to the Vestry House museum at a later date.

Two Wars and the Time Between

102a The scene in Richard's Place, off Hoe Street, in May 1918 after a German plane had dropped a 100kg. bomb which landed in the road. One hundred houses and shops were damaged. Two men, two women and two children were injured. The stock from many shops such as Allmans the gentleman's outfitters was damaged; shirts and ties were thrown out of the smashed windows and onto the pavement. This photograph shows the destruction of houses on the right side of Richard's Place, looking up to Hoe Street.

b Commercial buildings on the left-hand side facing Hoe Street include the *Rose and Crown* public house on the far right.

103 Food shortages were a part of life during the First World War, as this queue for potatoes demonstrates.

104 Walthamstow war memorial.

105 There were still open-top trams at the *Napier Arms* in 1921. Covered tops were not introduced until the late 1920s.

106 Thomas Munden ran a well-known off-licence on the corner of Carr and Brettenham Roads. The site was known as the Quadrant.

107 Evanston Avenue, Highams Park. During the 1920s and '30s new housing sprang up all around the pre-war core of Walthamstow.

LARKSHALL ROAD ESTATE, LARKSHALL RD., CHINGFORD.

Within 10 minutes' walk of Highams Park Station (L.N.E.R.), 20 minutes to Liverpool Street Station. 'Bus Terminus also at Highams Park Station. Chingford 'Buses within 2 minutes of Estate. Amid rural surroundings. Tennis Clubs and Sports Clubs are within ½ minute from the Estate. The Estate is built on a high position and set out under the Chingford Council's Town Planning Scheme and to their satisfaction, with a maximum of 12 houses to each acre of land. The Estate is quite close to open country and Epping Forest, together with two Golf Clubs.

FREEHOLD HOUSES from £725

£5 PART DEPOSIT, SECURES.

NO ROAD CHARGES LEGAL COSTS   **NO** STAMP DUTIES SURVEY FEES

GROUND FLOOR—OUTSIDE PORCH, DRAWING ROOM, DINING ROOM, and KITCHENETTE.

FIRST FLOOR—FRONT BEDROOM, SMALL FRONT BEDROOM, BACK BEDROOM, and BATHROOM.

OUTSIDE—All white W.C. with I.M. flap seat. Brick Coal Shed. 7 ft. Cement Paving. Cement Paving around front bays (for cleaning windows). Cement Path, cut-out imitation crazy paving.

The size of the plots average 20 ft. frontage and 120 ft. in depth. The Houses are of 20 ft. frontage. The front gardens are set at least 20 ft. back from the road. Every house has room for a garage, approached from the rear by a 10 ft. motor roadway leading direct to one of the roads.

THE ESTATE MANAGER attends at the Show House (or Estate Office) daily until dusk, including week-ends, and will be pleased to supply further information if required.

Telephones: SILVERTHORN 2371 (Estate Telephone) and WALTHAMSTOW 0801.

---

108 Larkshall Road Estate, advertised as being 'within ten minutes walk of Highams Park Station (L.N.E.R.)' was developed in the 1930s, just over the border in the Chingford section of Larkshall Road.

109 The High Street market, transformed by the new shopping parades, seen here in 1937. The Union Jack on the Palace Theatre is probably there to mark the coronation of George VI.

110 Chapel End in 1928. In spite of increasing development on all sides of the town between the wars there was still quite a rural flavour to parts of the district—in other parts ancient and modern were strangely juxtaposed.

111 Weston's cottages, Chingford Road, Chapel End in March 1932, next to a Victorian terrace.

112 The modern houses of Galesborough Avenue, looking towards the belt of trees at Beech Hall, 1933.

113 Wadham Farmhouse, Wadham Road, Chapel End in April 1932—a link with Walthamstow's agricultural past.

114 Salisbury Hall, Chapel End, in March 1932. E.J. Smith, an old inhabitant of Chapel End, remembered in 1952 that there had been a succession of farmers at the Hall: Halfhead (pig-breeders), Porter, Ferguson (who came down from Scotland with a trainload of stock and implements), Willis & Green, Kilpatrick and Howell. Salisbury Hall was not demolished until September 1952, although it had been in ruins for some years.

115 The last of the cornfield elms at the south end of Lyndhurst Road in May 1931. Wadham Farm is to the left. Annie R. Hatley, of the Walthamstow Antiquarian Society, writing in 1952, described the changes, 'By the 1930s most of the open spaces were built over, and the elms in the hedgerows were cut down and the fields which used to grow corn on the sunbathed slopes towards Chapel End quite quickly changed. They had been grazing-land and playing-fields, but a mushroom growth of "desirable residences" was soon up for sale'.

116 In Grove Road a remnant of the original lane could still be seen, at the junction of College Road, near the Leyton boundary, 1934.

117 Sun and shadow in old Shernhall Street in autumn 1934, with Victory House on the right. One could still glimpse the earlier Walthamstow of country houses and gentlemen's retreats seen on Rocque's map.

118 In 1928 some of the old houses in Wood Street remained, although converted in a haphazard way into shops. 'The property on the west side of Wood Street was mostly copyhold, which accounts for its being "funny"—some of the places had no back gardens, some had been taken over for modern premises, and some remained spacious. Copyhold property passed, by custom of the manor to the younger son, often only a boy. The widow, left without means, found it difficult to pay the annual "fine" to the lord of the manor. In addition there was a rental in many cases, and so new premises were sometimes erected on the copyhold land.' (*Across the Years*, ed. A. Hatley, 1953.)

119 Timbered houses in Jeffreys Square, Wood Street, seen from the rear in 1928. The area by Jeffreys Square was once known as 'Soapsuds Alley' because the people who lived there were able to have as much hot water as they liked from the brewery connected with the *Duke's Head*. As a result the area was always awash with soapsuds.

120 Mr. and Mrs. Sherman in the back garden of their home at no. 25 St Mary Road on the afternoon of 26 June 1930 with their cat Tibbles. During the 1930s back gardens were still the place where the larger part of many local people's leisure time was spent, since holidays away from home were few. Trellises were pinned up everywhere, and sheds and greenhouses constructed.

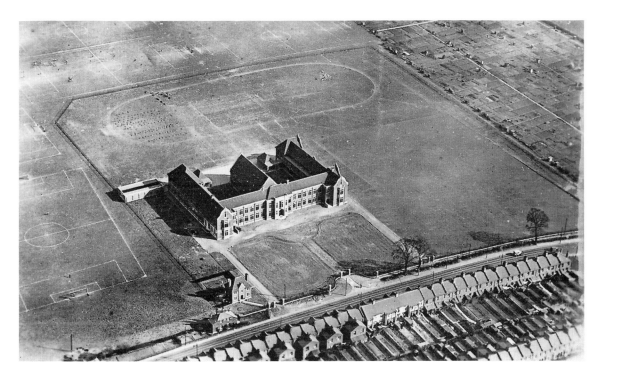

121   Aerial views of the spacious new building at Chapel End to which the Monoux School moved in 1927. From its early origins in the old almshouse block, near the parish church, the school moved to the Trinity schoolrooms in West Avenue in 1886, having been reorganised after a patchy existence which involved closure for about eight years. In 1916 the school was amalgamated with Grosvenor House Technical Institute boys' school, and Essex county council took over its running.

122 Charter Day, 10 October 1929—Walthamstow becomes a borough. The mayoral party and the Lord Privy Seal (the Rt. Hon. J.H. Thomas) who presented the Charter of Incorporation, are seen leaving the borough boundary at Ferry Lane Bridge for further ceremonies at the Town Hall.

123 Sir Courteney Warner (the Charter Mayor) receives the Royal Charter.

124 The Achille Serre works in the 1930s. This large factory belonged to a firm of dry-cleaners, once a nationally known name with premises all over the country. The Walthamstow Official Guide of 1961 states that 1,700 people were employed as dyers and cleaners.

125 The out-patients hall at the Connaught Hospital in 1931. The hospital on Orford Road had originally been a voluntary cottage hospital for children, started in 1877-8 in Brandon Road, off Wood Street. By 1880 it was at Salisbury Road, where it stayed until 1894. The gift of a large house, Holmcroft, on Orchard Road enabled the hospital to become both a children's and a general hospital.

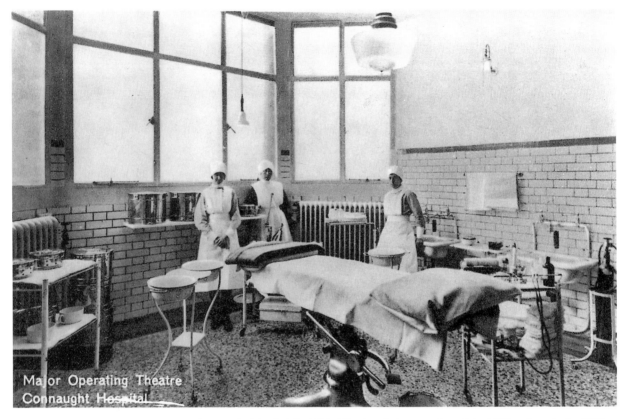

Major Operating Theatre
Connaught Hospital

126 The major operating theatre at Connaught Hospital in 1931. The hospital was enlarged in 1897 and again in 1903. In 1925 it had 50 beds. Additional wards were added in 1926-7. Previously named the Leyton, Walthamstow and Wanstead Hospital, it was renamed the Connaught after the Duchess of Connaught who had been patron since 1894.

Sun Ray Department ("Comely Bank")
Connaught Hospital

127 The sun-ray clinic in Comely Bank, Orford Road. This house was bought for hospital use in 1930, the year before this photograph was taken, enabling clinic facilities to be provided. It was realised in the 1930s that many children lacked vitamin C and that artificial sunlight was one way of remedying this.

128 The Avenue and the station in the suburb of Highams Park about 1911. The railway brought prosperity to this area. By the 1890s development had started, receiving a stimulus from the arrival of the British Xylonite Company from Homerton in 1898. This led to some reconstruction of the station, *c.*1900. By 1908 there were 5,000 residents in Highams Park, but no public house, although a good shopping area soon developed. Early terraced housing of 1899-1900 was decorated with plenty of ornament formed in white plaster on a rough cast base.

129 The level crossing at Highams Park, *c.*1929. Advertisement hoardings have been put up along the station fence. The Warner Company built solid terraces of houses, such as those between Chingford and Winchester Roads, and marked each of their properties with a 'W'. In the Edwardian era the principal builder was Mr. O.H. Watling. He erected red-brick homes with white stone facings, such as those in Beech Hall Road. By 1929 the inter-war housing boom had crept over the nearby Chingford border, and this had become the new growth area. However, to this day, much of it is still serviced by this station and the local shopping facilities, rather than those in Chingford town.

130 A waterside view at Highams Park lake; in 1920 there were some thirty acres of open space in this area under the control of the forest conservators. In 1891 the local board had contributed towards their purchase as an amenity for Walthamstow residents. The land had been offered for sale by Courteney Warner, the developer and later the Charter Mayor, perhaps as a way of making his estates more popular or maybe as a benevolent gesture. The lake itself occupied 14 acres, and boating was popular during the summer.

131 Hale End Road, Highams Park, on the other side of the railway line, showing the Regal Cinema, *c.*1938.

132 A group of children during the celebrations for the Coronation of King George VI and Queen Elizabeth in 1937.

133 Nocturnal scene at Walthamstow tram depot. These are the last days of tram operation, between October 1936 and June 1937. The trolleybuses in the background, under the depot roof, gradually replaced the trams.

134 Trolleybuses ready to go into service at Walthamstow depot. The first London Transport trolleybuses in the borough made their trial run from Woodford to the Manor House via Forest Road on 5 October 1936.

135 Old tramcars belonging to other systems were broken up behind Walthamstow station between 1936 and 1938.

136a Civil defence workers preparing for a fire-drill at the beginning of the Second World War.

b   Preparing to go into action.

c   Aiming the jet.

137 Happy faces at a street party organised to celebrate the end of the war in 1945. Note the clothing and hair fashions of the era.

SEASON 1956-57

SATURDAY, MARCH 16th

ISTHMIAN LEAGUE
(Senior Section)

WALTHAMSTOW AVENUE

v.

ROMFORD

KICK-OFF 3.0 p.m.

OFFICIAL PROGRAMME PRICE - - 3d.

NEXT HOME GAME :

Saturday, March 23rd—Senior XI v. Clapton

ISTHMIAN LEAGUE (Senior Section)   KICK-OFF 3.0 p.m.

138   This famous amateur soccer club originated in the late 1890s, when a master at Pretoria Avenue School, Mr. Parkin Davidson, founded Pretoria Avenue Old Boys as a means of keeping former pupils of the school in touch. The name was changed to Avenue United upon entry to the Walthamstow and District League in the season of 1900-1. It was not until 1903 that the present name was adopted. Walthamstow Avenue soon took part in some early continental tours, beginning as early as 1907. This became a club tradition and an annual event—the name of Walthamstow became well known in Holland, Luxembourg and Germany. After being disbanded during the First World War the club reformed in 1919 and joined the Spartan League. In 1921 it bought the ground on which it had been playing for some years—Green Pond Farm, and thereafter went from strength to strength. The F.A. Amateur Cup was won twice—once in 1952 when they beat Leyton 2-1, and again in 1961 when they beat West Auckland by the same score. Their finest hour was a draw with Manchester United, having reached the F.A. Cup sixth round.

BARKING · BECONTREE · ILFORD

LEYTONSTONE · EAST HAM · ROMFORD

WALTHAMSTOW AVENUE
Colours: Light and Dark Blue Hoops, White Shorts

RIGHT WING   LEFT WING

D. WELLS

2   3
D. CLARKE   T. FARRER

4   5   6
E. HARPER   S. PRINCE   G. LUCAS

7   8   9   10   11
R. GROVES   S. POOK   R. HOWITT   J. DUTCHMAN   K. DOWLER

Referee :
A. H. BEDFORD

TREBOR
EXTRA STRONG
PEPPERMINTS
The Whole Mint
Robertson & Woodcock Ltd
LONDON-CHESTERFIELD-WOODFORD

Linesmen :
G. D. EVANS and
R. H. EDWARDS

11   10   9   8   7
D. BOWNESS   C. WATTS   C. TIFFIN   B. BARBER   G. TILLYER

6   5   4
A. TAYLOR   P. JOLLY   R. FLEETWOOD

3   2
M. COOPER   N. APPLETON

1
P. GAMMAN

LEFT WING   RIGHT WING

ROMFORD
Colours: Royal Blue and Gold

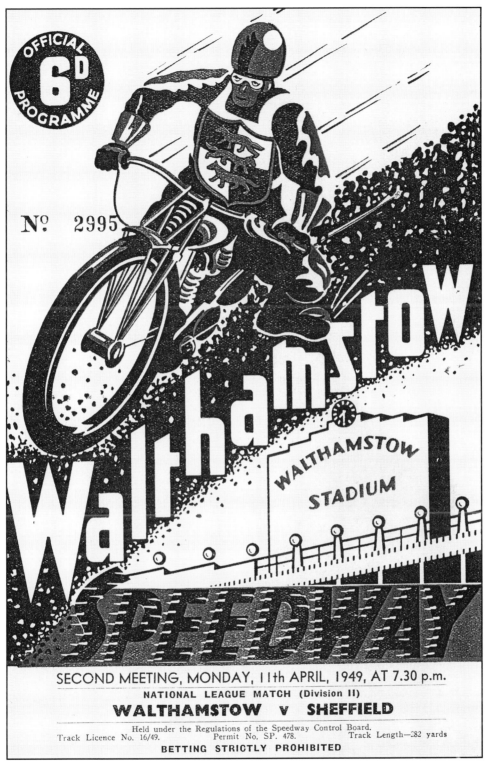

OFFICIAL
6^D
PROGRAMME

Nº 2995

Walthamstow

WALTHAMSTOW STADIUM

SPEEDWAY

SECOND MEETING, MONDAY, 11th APRIL, 1949, AT 7.30 p.m.
NATIONAL LEAGUE MATCH (Division II)
WALTHAMSTOW v SHEFFIELD
Held under the Regulations of the Speedway Control Board.
Track Licence No. 16/49.   Permit No. SP. 478.   Track Length—282 yards
BETTING STRICTLY PROHIBITED

139 Walthamstow Stadium was opened for greyhound racing in 1931. Critics laughed at Bill Chandler when he set up his own track in Walthamstow with two corrugated iron sheds for spectators. Yet before the end of the first year he was able to pull down the sheds and build a £50,000 stand. The running of the stadium remained a family affair until fairly recent times. After the Second World War speedway became an incredibly popular spectator sport. The 'Wolves', as Walthamstow's team were known, had many successes to their credit in the National League (Division Two). In 1952 the team were hoping to enter Division One as a result of the closure of the nearby West Ham team.

The Spirit of Walthamstow

140a The Rev. Eliezer Cogan ran a school in Essex Hall, Higham Hill at the beginning of the 19th century. It numbered amongst its pupils the future Prime Minister Benjamin Disraeli.

140b The remains of the former Manor House of Essex Hall are on the left of this picture. The outbuildings on the right were used by Dr. Cogan as schoolrooms, and the open courtyard provided the playground. This re-use of buildings is a common theme in Walthamstow's history—for instance the restarting of the Monoux School at the Trinity schoolrooms, West Avenue and the multiple uses of Vestry House.

141a William Morris is perhaps Walthamstow's most famous son. This bust by Henry Fehr was once exhibited at the public library, but was moved to Water House, his former home and now his museum. It hints at the grandeur of inspiration and intellect which he brought to bear in all his creative ventures.

141b An illustration from *The Life and Death of Jason,* one of the books published by William Morris's Kelmscott Press.

142 Sir John Simon represented Walthamstow as its M.P. between 1906 and 1918. He was to become Solicitor General in 1910 and, for a brief period between 1915 and 1916, Home Secretary.

143 A family celebration in about 1919. The members line up nonchalantly in the road outside their house together with friends. The photograph is by Pittman of Walthamstow.

144a At the end of the First World War the amazing vitality of the Walthamstow inhabitants revealed itself in hundreds of street parties celebrating peace and victory. This illustration shows the menfolk coming together, displaying a wide range of headgear. There are quite a number dressed in cloth cap and muffler. Some of the men had still not been released from the services; for others there was to be no return, the casualty rate in this war having been incredibly high.

144b The women pose for their picture. Notice the unbalanced proportion of females to males. Some children have also got into the frame.

144c Two children at their home prior to the celebration. These three pictures are the work of J.C. Collins, who is described as 'Photographer and Picture Framer' of 138 Northcote Road.

145 Brunswick Street celebrates the end of the First World War.

146 The table is ready for Coppermill Lane's victory tea in August 1919.

147 Victory tea in full progress in Leucha Road. The road was named after the developer's wife, Lady Leucha Warner.

148 The Fifth Walthamstow Jazz Band, or perhaps the local Scout group in costume before their carnival appearance in aid of the hospital and local charities—more Walthamstow enthusiasm and invention in aid of a good cause. Note the unmade pavement and roadway.

149 Some young pupils of Clark's College, Walthamstow. The college opened in April 1913 at Cleveland House, 285 Hoe Street, and this picture dates from 1916.

150 Class I, Pretoria Avenue School, Walthamstow. The school first opened on 24 August 1888, and the picture dates from February 1916.

151 An alert group from Standard 5A, North Central School, on 20 September 1914, in a very orderly classroom with books in one cupboard, chemicals in another and a large number of framed prints and photographs on the walls. At the beginning of the century standards in Walthamstow schools had not been high, but by 1914 they were beginning to rise.

152 St Mary's convent school, 1931.

153 A religious procession starts out from the Roman Catholic Church of Our Lady and St George. This stands on the site of a small stone building which was built in the 1820s when Cardinal Wiseman lived at Shern Hall (now Shernhall Street). This and the following three photographs show the procession moving along the streets near the church.

It is an exciting day for the children as their proud parents watch their progress.

154 The United Methodist church, Highams Park. This was one of the churches which helped to create communities from the new inhabitants by organising clubs, events and self-help.

155 A large turnout for a summer outing organised by Church Hill Sunday school in 1910. Such events were eagerly awaited throughout the year, and relieved the hardship of many children's everyday lives. The photograph is by Owen of Wood Street.

156 A keen Salvation Army band from the Walthamstow Citadel, April 1912. In the second row from the back, third from the right is Mr. Risly. The backdrop of extensive trelliswork may be behind Matioli's studio, opposite the Citadel in the High Street, as the photograph is the work of Mr. Matioli.

157a-f The organisation of the Special Police in Walthamstow was first-rate. Walthamstow people were always ready to give their service to such organisations. This set of six pictures shows recruits being assessed in a first-aid test which comprised bandaging and stretcher-work. The pictures were taken shortly after the end of the First World War.

Although this was a test of medical expertise and ability to deal with emergencies, the photographer has captured these posed scenes resembling exercises in military drill.

The hapless 'casualty' on the stretcher was hoisted aloft in a ceremony more like the changing of the Guard.

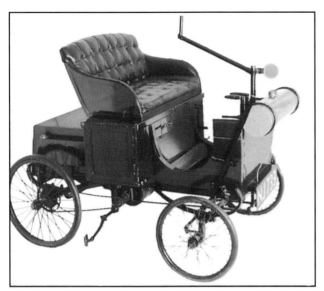

158 The Bremer car. The pioneering spirit of Walthamstow led to the development, between 1892 and 1894, of a very early British car with an internal combustion engine, which is sometimes held to be the first in Britain. Fred Bremer and his wife were often to be seen proceeding along Woodford New Road, with a runner in front carrying the statutory red flag.

159a Walthamstow Palace Theatre staged most kinds of theatrical production during its lifetime (1903-54). As well as famous music-hall stars such as Marie Lloyd, Harry Lauder and Chirgwin there were plays, musicals and variety shows. When Adney Payne built the Palace Theatre of Varieties, to give it its full title, early entrance fees were 4d. in the pit and 2d. in the gallery. Rotten fruit from the market outside was often directed at unsuccessful performers!

159b Advertisements for the Palace—Juvenile and Novelty bands were an American import to variety theatres in Britain.

WALTHAMSTOW PALACE THEATRE

Box office open 10 a.m. to 10 p.m.   HIGH STREET, E.17   Reserve your seats by telephone

Telephone: Walthamstow 0040

The World's Finest Musical, Dramatic and Vaudeville Entertainments Weekly

NEXT WEEK

A SPECIALLY ARRANGED

VAUDEVILLE PROGRAMME

INCLUDING

TEDDY JOYCE'S JUVENILE BAND

VARIETY AT ITS BEST

MANAGER'S SPECIAL GIFT NIGHT WEDNESDAY — Second House	CARNIVALS THURS. & FRI. — Second Houses

In the interest of Public Health this Theatre is Disinfected throughout with JEYES' FLUID

WALTHAMSTOW PALACE THEATRE

Box Office open 10 a.m. to 10 p.m.   HIGH STREET, E.17   Reserve your seats by telephone LARkswood 3040

6.40   TWICE NIGHTLY   8.55

Manager ... ... R. B. CALDWELL

The World's Finest Musical, Dramatic and Vaudeville Entertainments Weekly

FORTHCOMING ATTRACTIONS

MONDAY NEXT

FRANK H. FORTESCUE
presents
The Greatest of all Comedy Revues

THE RENT RACKET

Laughs !   Screams]!   Yells !   Don't Miss It !   Revue at its Best !

Star Cast includes

WAL BUTLER   **THE DECORATORS**
THE LITTLE COMEDIAN   THE FAMOUS JERRY BUILDERS

LYNDA LAYNE, PAT FORUM, RITA PAGE, GEORGE RUTHERFORD
TED ANDREWS, THE 3 RACKETEERS, JACK KENRICK, IDA MARGO
REG ADAIR   THE MARGO YOUNG LADIES   BETTY EVANS

MONDAY, AUGUST 21st, 1939	MONDAY, AUGUST 28th, 1939
THE OVALTINEYS with FULL SUPPORTING COMPANY	MAY-WEST PRODUCTIONS present **ROOM FOR TWO** (From the Garrick Theatre, W.) This Show had a Long and Successful Run in the West End

Book Your Seats Early.   No Extra.   Box Office Open 10 a.m. to 10 p.m.

The Management cannot be responsible for the absence of any artistes through illness or any other circumstance

In the interests of Public Health this Theatre is disinfected throughout with JEYES' FLUID

159c In 1939 Comedy Revues were all the rage, influenced by West End successes. The Ovaltineys were originally part of a radio advertisement

160 (*above*) Brookscroft in Forest
Road was typical of the old houses
which once dotted the landscape of
Walthamstow. In 1930 it was the
headquarters of the Walthamstow Child
Welfare Society.

161 (*above*) The Lea, as the borough's western boundary, has always imparted some of its atmosphere to the town. This print depicts the view from Lea Bridge at the end of the 19th century.

162 (*left*) The Lea at Clapton in the earlier decades of the century. Similar to its stretch through Walthamstow— angling and boating were favourite pastimes here.

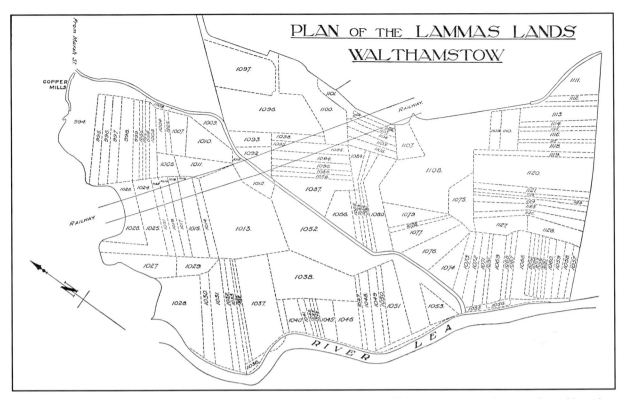

163 The Lammas lands from the tithe map of 1842. These meadows were held in common over the centuries, with each local householder having a portion allocated to him either by rotation or by the drawing of lots. The lands were carefully enclosed and protected soon after Christmas until the crop, whether hay or corn, was reaped in the summer, perhaps around Lammas, 1 August.

164 The keeper's cottage and 'Sale' at Highams Park. This scene gives a flavour of forest Walthamstow at the turn of the century. The 'Sale' woodland takes its name from the Old English for willow tree—'sealh'.

165 Beating the Bounds. The itinerary of the Walthamstow Antiquarian Society's tour of the boundaries in September 1964. The ceremony was recorded in 1711, and was revived for the Festival of Britain in 1951.

WALTHAMSTOW ANTIQUARIAN SOCIETY

1914   1964

CEREMONY OF

BEATING THE BOUNDS

SATURDAY, 26th SEPTEMBER 1964

STARTING AT WALTHAMSTOW MUSEUM AT 11 a.m.

OCCASIONAL
PUBLICATION No. 5

PROGRAMME
PRICE **6** D.

THE BOROUGH OF WALTHAMSTOW

NUMBERS REFER TO BOUNDARY POSTS & STOPS

PROGRAMME

(Times approximate)

OPENING CEREMONY at Vestry House Museum in the presence of His Worship the Mayor of Walthamstow and the Town Clerk	11 a.m.
Leave for Ferry Boat Inn in coaches at ...	11.15 a.m.
POST No. 1* Ceremony at Ferry Boat Inn	11.30 a.m.
Walking party by the towpath to Lea Bridge and coach party via Markhouse Road... ...	11.45 a.m.
POST No. 2* Ceremony at S.W. corner of the Borough (grid ref. 354871)	1.0 p.m.
Leave Lea Bridge	1.15 p.m.
POST No. 3 Ceremony near Forest School	1.30 p.m.
POST No. 4* Ceremony near "Napier Arms"	1.50 p.m.
POST No. 5* Chingford Lane/Charter Road (not stopping)	2.10 p.m.
POST No. 6* Ceremony at Chingford Hatch bridge	2.15 p.m.
POST No. 7* Ceremony in Larkshall Road	2.35 p.m.
POST No. 8 Ceremony at Ching River bridge on the North Circular Road	3.0 p.m.
POST No. 9 Ceremony on the footpath from Sinnott Road to Tottenham	3.30 p.m.
Arrive back at Vestry House Museum ...	4.0 p.m.

* Actual fixed boundary posts

166 Mentioned as a key point on the boundary through the years was the old *Ferry Boat*. This engraving of 1836 shows it, along with Hillyers (wooden) bridge over the river Lea and the *Ferry Boat* inn.

167 The *Ferry Boat* inn, earlier this century. The manor courts were once held here.

168 An iron boundary post dating from 1812 and situated near the Eagle pond. It was erected by Viscount Maynard of Walthamstow Toni manor.

169 We have returned to the heart of old Church End, Walthamstow. It is a great credit to the local authority, the Walthamstow Antiquarian Society as well as to the people of the town that this area has been preserved and made special. The old village is unique in a London suburb in retaining so many of its old buildings, clustered around the parish church.

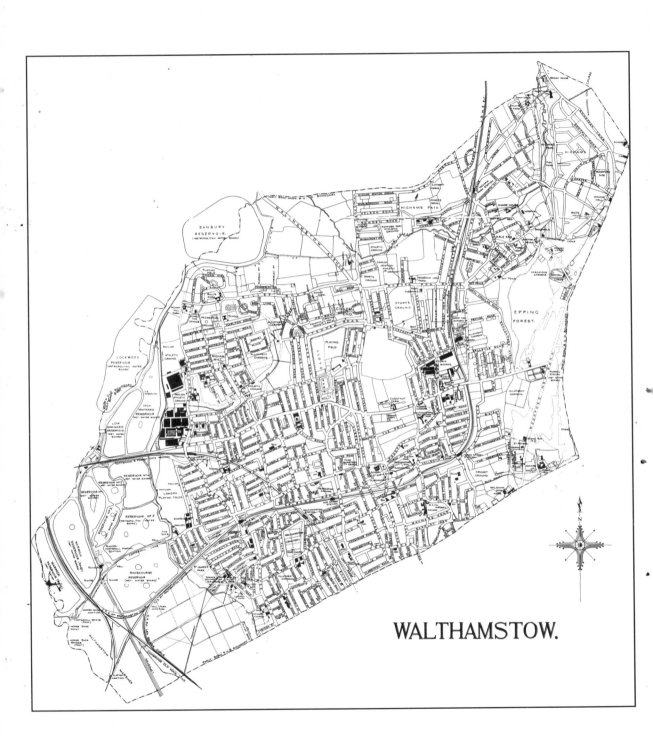

WALTHAMSTOW.